Senior Editor Jane Yorke
Art Editor Toni Rann
Designer Jane Coney
Editorial Director Sue Unstead
Art Director Colin Walton
Photography Stephen Oliver
Additional photography Michael Dunning, Karl Shone
Series Consultant Neil Morris

This is a Dorling Kindersley Book
published by Random House, Inc.

First American edition, 1990

Library of Congress Cataloging-in-Publication Data
My first look at opposites.
    p. cm.
 Summary: Photographs depict such opposites as big and little,
up and down, full and empty, in and out, and open and closed.
  ISBN 0-679-80620-2
  1. English language – Synonyms and antonyms – Juvenile
literature.
[1. English language – Synonyms and antonyms.] I. Random House
(Firm)
PE1591.M88 1990
428.1 – dc20
89-63093 CIP AC

Manufactured in Italy 1 2 3 4 5 6 7 8 9 10

Phototypeset by Flairplan Phototypesetters Ltd, Ware, Hertfordshire
Reproduced in Hong Kong by Bright Arts
Printed in Italy by L.E.G.O.

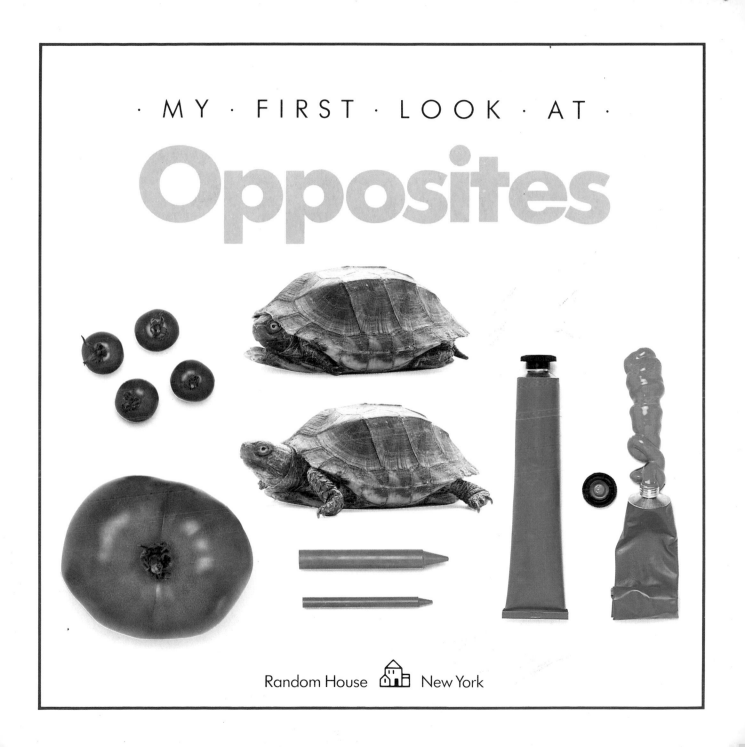

· MY · FIRST · LOOK · AT ·

Opposites

Random House ⌂ New York

Big and little

shoes

leaves

cars

crabs

tomatoes

dolls

Thick and thin

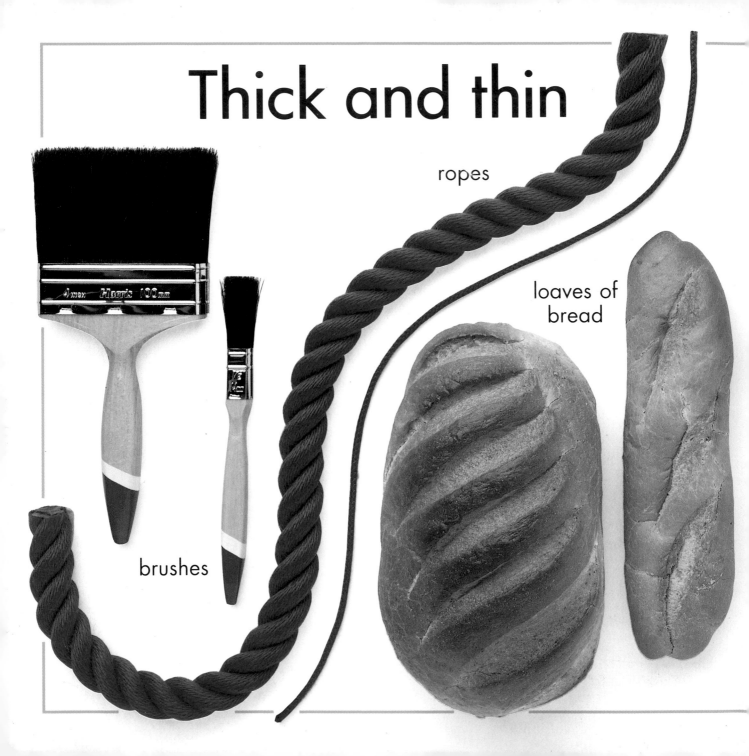

ropes

loaves of
bread

brushes

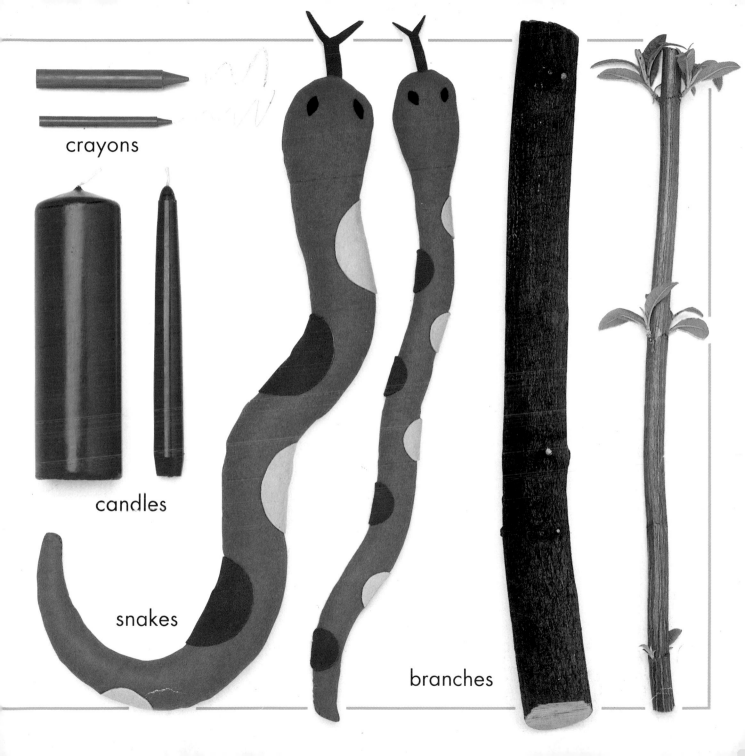

crayons

candles

snakes

branches

Long and short

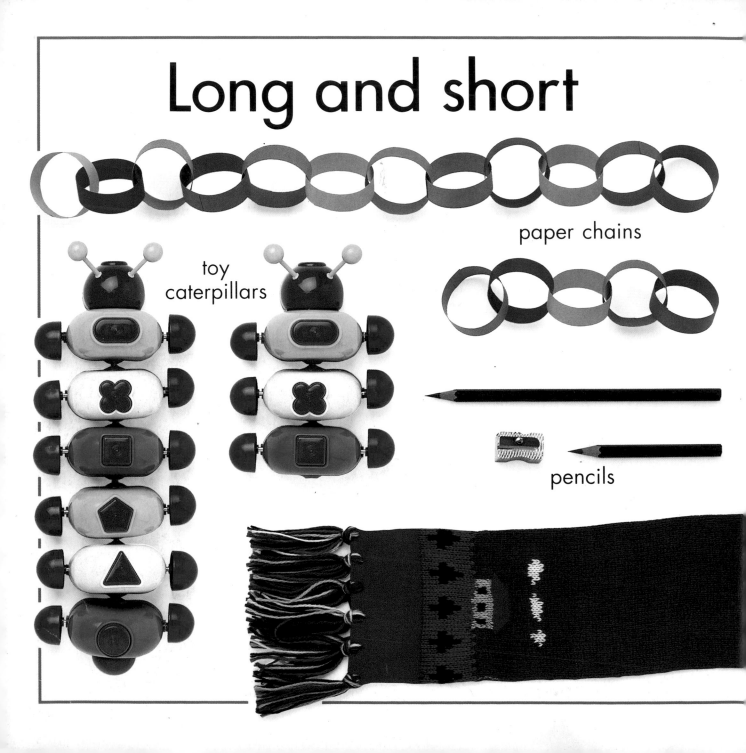

paper chains

toy
caterpillars

pencils

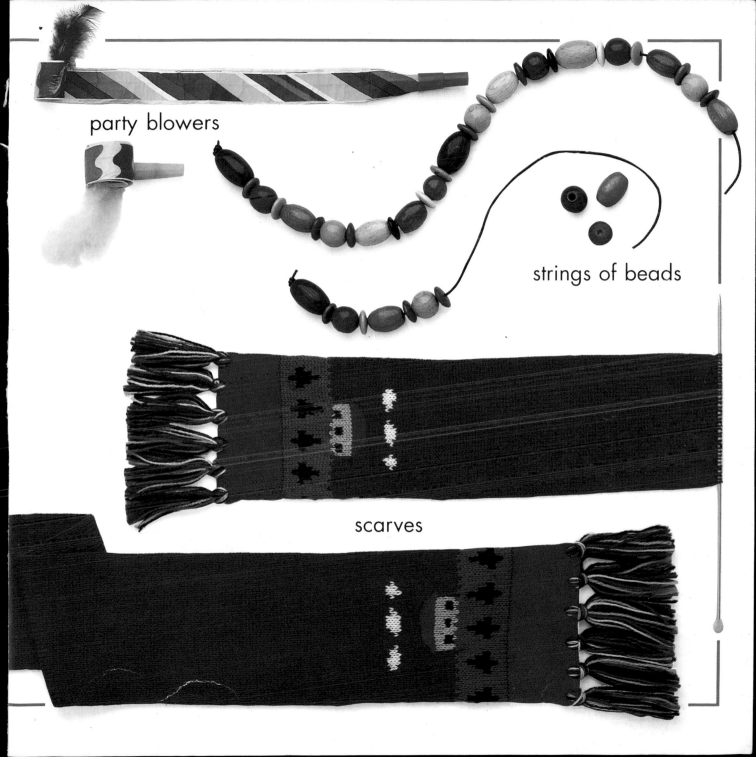

party blowers

strings of beads

scarves

In and out

pilot

sandcastle

turtle

snail

jack-in-the-box

Up and down

crane

puppet

fire engine

train

Full and empty

cookie tin

bird's nest

toy box

tube of paint

bowl of
fruit

glass of
punch

candy jar

Front and back

clock

tiger

car

puzzle
piece

playing
card

coat

wooden doll

Open and closed

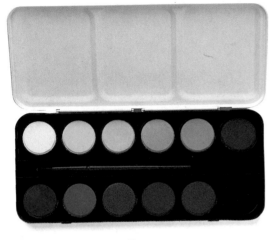

paint box

toolbox

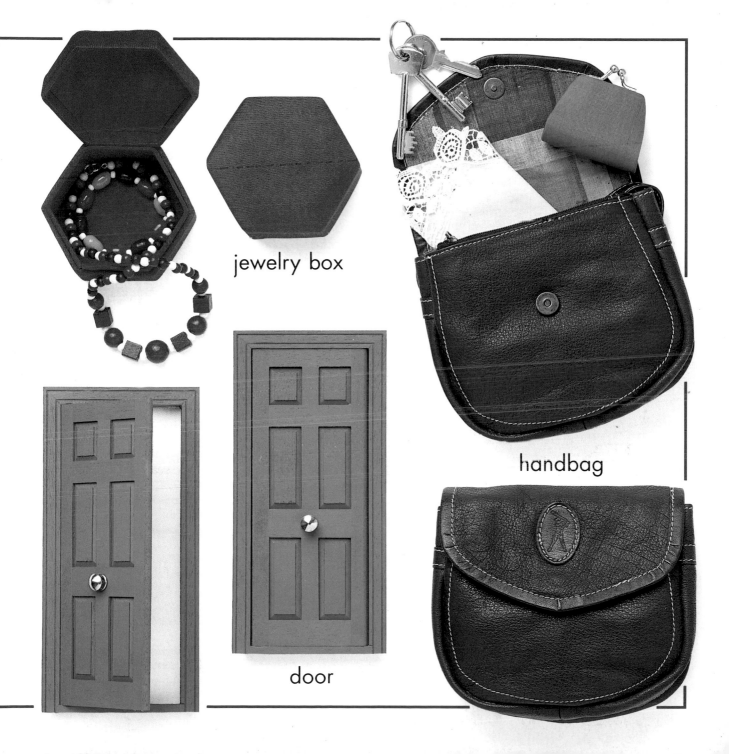

jewelry box

door

handbag